D1512010

COOL CATS

COOL CATS

EDITED BY

J. C. SUARÈS

TEXT BY

JANA MARTIN

PHOTO RESEARCH BY

KATRINA FRIED

WELCOME

NEW YORK

Published in 1998 by Welcome Enterprises, Inc.
588 Broadway, New York, NY 10012
(212) 343-9430 FAX (212) 343-9434

Distributed in the U.S. by Stewart, Tabori & Chang
a division of U.S. Media Holdings, Inc.
115 West 18th Street, New York, NY 10011

Copyright © 1998 J.C. Suarès
Text copyright © 1998 Jana Martin
Additional copyright information on page 80

All rights reserved, including the right of reproduction
in whole or in part in any form.

NOTICE: Every effort has been made to locate the copyright
owners of the materials used in the book. Please let us
know if an error has been made, and we will make any
necessary changes in subsequent printings.

Library of Congress Card Catalog Number: 98-85635
ISBN: 0-941807-21-5

Printed and bound in Italy by Arnoldo Mondadori Editore
10 9 8 7 6 5 4 3 2 1

PAGE 1:

DONNA RUSKIN
SEBASTIAN YAWNING,
YONKERS, NEW YORK, 1988

"This is my cat Sebastian at home. He's a
silver-spotted, tabby, oriental shorthair."

PAGE 2:

JAN RIETZ
LOOKING FOR FOOD,
SKÅNE, SWEDEN, 1995

"My friend Åke and I were traveling in a county
called Skåne, in the southernmost part of Sweden.
We'd stopped in the grass for a picnic when this
little cat came over. He was very young, very
hungry, and very persistent. We thought perhaps
he'd been traveling with a family and had
somehow lost track of them when they stopped
here for lunch. We gave him some milk, and some
ham, which he devoured. Unfortunately, we
couldn't take him with us. I hope the family he
was with came back to look for him, because he
was a terrific cat. You could tell."

PAGE 5:

ANONYMOUS
STOOP CAT,
NEW YORK CITY, 1940s

With one ear to traffic and the other to
the sounds inside the rowhouse beside it,
this young domestic shorthair rests
in a patch of light on a city stoop.

PAGE 8-9:

DAVID McENERY
BLACKJACK,
REDONDO BEACH, CALIFORNIA, 1994

"This cat lives on a boat with someone, and he
just hangs out on the dock."

'd never seen him before, but there he was, sleeping at the foot of the bed when I woke up at dawn: a large orange cat with a red collar.

In Connecticut, I often slept with the windows of my first-floor bedroom open, and I had expected a visitor or two sooner or later (a baby skunk once walked in the front door). I thought it would be a squirrel, or a bat perhaps, but not somebody else's orange cat.

In time, the cat woke up and devoured a can of tuna. He cleaned himself from head to toe, played with a black sock and suddenly disappeared as mysteriously as he had shown up.

He showed up the next night, however, and the night after that. He'd let out a short, expressive gurgle as he'd come through the window. And then it would be the same routine: sleep, tuna, toilet, play, and poof! Gone.

It didn't matter if it rained or snowed. He'd show up anyway, sometimes soaking wet. Once, when he appeared all bloodied from a fight, I took him to the vet for emergency care. It was too embarrassing to admit that he wasn't my cat, so I made up some bogus answers on that little form they ask you to fill out. Age: 3, name: Mike, neutered: no, last visit: last year.

The vet found two kinds of worms, gum disease, a rotten tooth and several open cuts. Final price tag: $644 (check or cash, and we accept credit cards).

Mike and I got to be good friends, quite comfortable in our nightly routine. But the same questions kept nagging me: whose cat was he? Who bought the red collar? Where did he spend his days? Did he live in a house nearby, and was his owner as fond of him as I was? At night, did they miss him?

I tried following him into the woods in the morning, but I always lost track of him. It would be months before I got my answer. One day, while shopping in town about two miles away, I noticed a big orange cat with a red collar sleeping amongst the one-gallon cans of olive oil in the window of Orlofsky's Groceries. There was no question it was Mike.

It was several more weeks before I decided to tell Mr. Orlofsky about his two-timing cat. Not an easy task:

how do you explain to somebody that you've been sleeping with his cat?

Mr. Orlofsky listened to my story with great interest, looked back at the sleeping cat (who never betrayed the fact that he knew me) and said, "stop feeding him and he'll stop bothering you."

Of course, I fed him just like before. And spent some high-quality nights with him. When I moved out of the house I made sure the new tenant would be one who appreciated the night visitor. And by the way, I never needed to find out the cat's real name from Mr. Orlofsky, since he answered to Mike right away.

—J.C. Suarès

ABOVE:

DONNA RUSKIN
GREENVILLE ARMS TABBY,
CATSKILLS, NEW YORK, 1991

"This shorthaired tabby, resident cat at a bed-and-breakfast in
the Catskill Mountains, thinks nothing of lying straight across the
path of oncoming guests. His excuse may be the sunshine, but does
he get a kick out of watching guests step gingerly around him?"

RIGHT:

MIKAEL BERTMAR
CAT AND SHADOW,
GOTHENBORG, SWEDEN, 1990

"One very sunny summer day, I was walking through a
nice Gothenborg neighborhood. It's an area with both smaller
villas and bigger houses, where everything is very tidy. I saw
this cat stalking around, accompanied by his wilder shadow,
and I thought, here's somebody's ordinary housecat feeling just
like a tiger. After I took the picture the cat came up and
rubbed against my leg, and seemed domestic once again. I like to
think he was thanking me for sharing his secret life."

My cat Aretha hates loud rock, but she loves the sound of a good song. If I go to the piano and play something she likes, she'll come over to listen. She prefers something low-key, but she'll really get into the blues if she's in the right mood. She doesn't mind guitar, though she prefers it acoustic. And she hates the drums. I had a piano student who liked her a lot, and he used to bring her treats, like a can of tuna or sardines. After Aretha devoured the entire thing, she'd get up on top of the piano and roll over onto her side to listen to him play. She'd loll on top of that piano and purr for an hour while my student practiced his rolling bass lines.

S.A. SLIM, MUSICIAN, NEW ORLEANS

RIGHT:
DAVID McENERY
HIGH C,
LOS ANGELES, CALIFORNIA, 1994
"This is our cat, Lovejoy. He'd fallen asleep inside the guitar case, and when he woke up, he gave a big yawn. Anything we leave laying around, Lovejoy adopts and falls asleep in it."

LEFT:

**UPI PHOTOGRAPHER
O SOUL O MEOW,
BIRMINGHAM, ENGLAND, 1961**

"The Birmingham man who owned this
cat declared him '50 percent Siamese
and a 100 percent musical snob.'"

ABOVE:
CLAUDIA GORMAN
TALKING KITTY,
PLEASANT VALLEY, NEW YORK, 1994

"Curry always has something to say about everything. This
time, he was complaining about the lack of decor in his box."

RIGHT:
CLAUDIA GORMAN
HANGIN' IN THERE,
PLEASANT VALLEY, NEW YORK, 1993

"Cassie, who's Curry's mother, was a kitten here. She was experiencing
a bout of Spring fever, and was determined to get outside."

When my husband and I lived in a fifth-floor apartment in New York City, my Abyssinian cat, Ana Cleopatra, used to sit at the living room window and watch the birds, her teeth chattering with excitement. The window had an air conditioner in it. What we didn't realize was that the vent on one side of the air conditioner was loose. One afternoon we came home, and there was no sign of Ana. We searched the house, but no cat. Then we saw the hole next to the air conditioner, the vent pushed to one side. Our hearts sank. We thought, if Ana went after a bird and forgot she was so high up in the air, how could she survive?

We ran downstairs with heavy hearts, expecting the worst. My husband started calling her name, not even knowing where to begin looking. But as it turned out, Ana jumped from the bushes straight into his arms. She'd probably been wondering how the heck was she going to get back home. Shaken, we brought her upstairs. Miraculously, nothing was broken—she was just a little a dazed for a day or so. And then she went right back to watching the birds and chattering her teeth.

TANIA GARCIA, DESIGNER, WESTCHESTER

RIGHT:
ANONYMOUS
CAUGHT, PLACE AND DATE UNKNOWN
A solitary alley cat freezes for just a quick
moment, holding its trophy in its mouth.

PRECEDING PAGES:
DAVID McENERY
CATVILLE TOURS,
SANTA MONICA BEACH, 1994

"There was a guy on the Santa Monica Beach for
a while who lived in a bus, and travelled with
some twenty-five cats. They were very
accustomed to bus life."

RIGHT:
MARY ELLEN MARK
JULIA SWEENEY,
NEW YORK CITY, 1996

"This photograph was done for *The New Yorker*.
Julia Sweeney loves cats. This is not her cat,
it's a model, but she loved it anyway."

OVERLEAF:
MARY ELLEN MARK
ROBIN QUIVERS AND HER CAT,
NEW YORK, 1995

Robin Quivers, radio personality of *The Howard
Stern Show* and *Private Parts* costar, relaxes in
her New York City apartment with her cat.

Batty, my cat, is enormous, but she moves pretty fast. The
only thing is that she sometimes gets stuck in places. My
friend came over with her dog, and Batty hates dogs. First
she puffed herself up to twice her size, which made her look
absolutely obese. But she thought she looked really tough.
Then, when the dog didn't get scared, she charged. The dog
didn't move. So at the last minute Batty veered away and
dashed behind the armchair. Somehow she got herself
wedged in there, though I didn't know it. I just thought she
was hiding. Hours later, my friend and the dog had gone,
and I heard a plaintive little meow coming from behind the

chair. There was Batty, stuck in the funniest position, all four
paws off the ground and her belly stuck between the back of
the chair and the wall. She had kept her cool until the dog
was gone rather than admit she needed help.

DEANNA CHUI, LAWYER, BROOKLYN

RIGHT:
ANONYMOUS
WHITE CAT, U.S., 1950s
At home on the moving edge of a rolling
wooden ball, this white cat keeps its cool.

Kook, my Siamese kitten, has prevented me from getting
any sleep for the last three weeks. He has discovered that
he has claws. At around midnight, just when I am trying to
finally fall asleep, he gets wild. He likes to free-climb the
curtains all the way up to the rods and then try to kill the
curtain rings. I hear them rattling under his busy paws, and
then I know I'm in for it. The next thing that happens is that
he comes flying through the air, having propelled himself
off a curtain rod, and lands on my bed—usually right on
top of me, with all four paws extended. He also likes to
leap onto my shirt and then rappel down my pant leg.
Serves me right, I suppose, for those long hours I leave him
alone when I go teach my slow fellow-humans how to climb.

CARL STERLING, CLIMBING INSTRUCTOR, BOSTON

RIGHT:
DAVID McENERY
HER SURROGATE, BEAULIEU, FRANCE, 1996
"Claude, our neighbor, had adopted a small Siamese
kitten whose mother had been hit by a car. I was visiting
Claude one afternoon when I noticed the kitten had taken
a fancy to the cat statue in the window. 'Perhaps,' said
Claude, 'it replaces her mother.'"

OVERLEAF:
KARL BADEN
RADAR CAT, RHODE ISLAND, 1993
"At a cat show, one of the problems is finding a way to
integrate foreground and background. But this cat
obviously didn't care a whit about the background."

ABOVE:

ANONYMOUS

FOCUS, U.S., 1950s

Is there a mouse at the other end?
An inquiring tabby takes a gander at
the world through a long lens.

RIGHT:

TOM SALYER/UPI

PRINCESS SIX-TOES,

KEY WEST, FLORIDA, 1982

At twenty-three, this cat is the only one remaining
(out of at least fifty) from the days when the Key
West house she lives in was owned by writer Ernest
Hemingway. Her domain is the library; her favorite
place is above the Royal typewriter. According to
the housekeeper, "She's the reigning queen."

LEFT:

**JOHN DRYSDALE
PEEK-A-BOO,
LONDON, ENGLAND, 1990**

"The pianist for a London toddlers'
dancing class used to bring her
cat, which always distracted the
kids. The cat, on the other
hand, never seemed too interested.
One afternoon, while it was groom-
ing itself — typically oblivious to
the goings-on — one little girl
decided an inverted view of the cat
was far more interesting than an
arabesque. True to form, the cat
ignored the entire spectacle."

ABOVE:

KARL BADEN

CAT AND FORK, BOSTON, 1992

"You'd think that this cat wore a bib for mealtime.
Actually a lot of long-haired cats wear bibs at cat
shows, so they won't lick themselves and mess
up their hair before they're judged."

RIGHT:

ROBIN SCHWARTZ

CHANEL, NEW YORK CITY, 1996

"This lion-cut calico Persian named Chanel is a veteran
show cat. She comes to Madison Square Garden every
year from Florida, where she lives with Lise, her owner,
who's a groomer. Chanel is thirteen years old. I think
older cats have more of a sense of laissez-faire than
younger ones. They have a certain dignity about them
that comes from having been around the block."

RIGHT:

NED ROSEN
ABYSSINIAN AND ACTRESS,
HOLLYWOOD, 1992

"While I was photographing Susan Sullivan, an
actress who was recently seen in *My Best Friend's
Wedding*, her cat, an Abyssinian, managed to
both stay at arm's length and be in every picture.
One of the tricks you pick up in L.A."

PAGE 56:

FRED SOMERS, UPI
MY DOMAIN,
WILMINGTON, DELAWARE, 1980s

On a cold afternoon, this short-haired
tabby stands in the gap of a picket fence.

PAGE 57:

JOHAN WILLNER
CAT WITH MURDEROUS EYES,
NEW YORK, 1996

"While in New York in June, I was walking along
Sixth Avenue. Sitting on the sidewalk in front of a deli
was this cat. I guess he belonged to the deli owner.
When I bent down to take his picture, he came over to
me, curious about what I was doing. He looks like a
mean cat, but he was really quite nice."

ABOVE:

KARL BADEN

LOVER, BOSTON, 1992

"This cat was rolling around, trying to seduce me.
Fortunately, or maybe unfortunately, I resisted."

RIGHT:

ANN FINNELL

SAM, NEW YORK CITY, 1997

"Sam, our domestic shorthair tabby, knows when I'm
taking his picture. He likes to get into as feline a position as possible, preferably on my favorite armchair,
and do a little on-camera demonstration of how impos-
sibly supple and adorable cats are — as opposed to
people, who can't quite stretch out the same way."

RIGHT:

JOHN DRYSDALE
KITTENS PREFER DONKEYS,
WALES, 1976

"As their mother didn't show any interest in them, these kittens left the comforts of the farmhouse for a pile of straw bales in the stable. Soon they graduated to the warm back of the donkey, who didn't seem to mind at all."

OVERLEAF:

ANN FINNELL
SAM & DAVE,
NEW YORK CITY, 1997

"Dave, who as you can see, is very handsome in his gray and white tuxedo, is the older (and more conniving) member of Sam and Dave, the duo we adopted from Bide-a-Wee in 1995. We'd planned to adopt a little female kitten but instead wound up with two full-grown males. What happened is that we were walking through the shelter's adoption area when Dave stuck his paw through the bars of his cage and touched our hands, as if to say, 'Here I am, what took you so long?' He was irresistible. By the time we found out he was part of a package deal, it was too late. Cats do this. No matter what your plans are, it's really up to them."

ABOVE:

ROBIN SCHWARTZ
SONY,
NORTH BERGEN, NEW JERSEY, 1997

"Sony, a very pretty cream Persian,
likes to sit on her behind like a person.
She's about three years old."

ABOVE:
ROBIN SCHWARTZ
CHINA,
RUTHERFORD, NEW JERSEY, 1996
"China, a domestic shorthair, was very
shy the whole time I was around.
Here she's about two years old."

My black and white cat, Roland, adopted me. He's so handsome—with enormous yellow eyes and a majestic ruff around his neck—that I just had to take him in. I was eating breakfast on my front porch when he came galloping out of nowhere, obviously very hungry. The problem was, at that point, that I had three adolescent dogs who were very disobedient, and a teenage son, and I was in the habit of raising my voice a bit. As in "Hey! Get your nose out of the refrigerator!" Or "Off the couch with those filthy feet!" Well, the dogs are used to it, and my son forgave me too, though he suggested I try a certain illegal herb to relax. But Roland immediately let me know that he, being a cat, would not tolerate such outbursts. One day I caught him sharpening his claws on a chair leg and yelled "Bad cat! Stop that now!" Instead Roland just turned his head and gave me a piercing stare. It was as if he were saying, "Excuse me? Just whom do you think you're talking to?"

LISE KLAMMER, NURSE, AMSTERDAM

RIGHT:
DAVID McENERY
STREET OF CATS, DINAN, FRANCE, 1994
"There is a street in Dinan that leads down to the port.
It's a very old street, twisting and cobblestoned. I
think everyone who lives on it must have a cat,
because they are everywhere you look. I noticed this
one peering at me as I took an afternoon walk."

ABOVE:

**UNIDENTIFIED
CLEVER CAT,
NEW YORK, 1940s**

This clever tuxedo-patterned cat, according
to his trainer A. Coxe, can juggle with
figures up to six, and can add, multiply,
and subtract. He gives his answers by
sitting down on the right square.

RIGHT:

**UNIDENTIFIED
GOING THROUGH HOOPS,
NEW YORK, 1940s**

Trainer A. Coxe and his assistant
hold the hoops while a spotted
shorthair leaps neatly through them.

LEFT:

ANONYMOUS DOCK CAT, NEW ENGLAND

As familiar with boats and water as he is with land, a burly fisherman's cat transverses the rowboats on his way in for the night.

OVERLEAF:

UPI PHOTOGRAPHER SWIMMER THE KITTEN, SANTA MONICA, CALIFORNIA, 1956

Ten-year-old Donna Pick helped her two-and-a-half-month-old tabby kitten get used to the water by pulling her on a raft. Soon the cat was leaping off a diving board and coming along for morning laps.

71

RIGHT:

**ANONYMOUS
BLIMP,
NEW YORK, 1919**

Airshipman William Ballantyne
smuggles his cat on board the
dirigible when he goes to work.

7 4

My friend who's extremely plump has a cat who out of sym-
pathy became quite large as well, until the two of them
were just enormous. The cat, though, is very proud of his
bulk and carries it quite well, while his owner, on the other
hand, seems quite embarrassed for himself.

VIVIEN GOLDMAN, MUSIC WRITER,
NEW YORK AND LONDON

RIGHT:
MARJORIE LUNDEN
I'M READY, STOCKHOLM, 1996
"When you point a camera at my cat, he poses. Cats are
much more aware than we think they are. How else do
you explain a cat who walks into a photographer's house
and becomes her best model, always aware of the lens?"

OVERLEAF:
PALMER M. PEDERSEN
FOLLOW ME, MONTANA, 1955
Neighboring rancher and amateur photographer Palmer
Pedersen caught this seven-member procession walking
along the crest of a Montana hill. Like kittens following
their mother, these cats stay close to their elderly owner.

PHOTO CREDITS

Cover, 1, 12, 24-25, 30, 31: © Donna Ruskin
Back cover, 5, 16-17, 27, 29, 43, 48, 49, 56, 70-71, 73,
    75, 78-79: UPI/Corbis-Bettmann
2: © Jan Rietz/Tiofoto
8-9, 15, 23, 35, 36-37, 45, 67: © David McEnery
13: © Mikael Bertmar/Tiofoto
18, 19: © Claudia Gorman
21: Corbis-Bettmann
32-33: © Lars Peter Roos/Tiofoto
34: © Michael Nichols, Magnum Photos Inc.
39, 40-41: © Mary Ellen Mark
46-47, 52, 58: © Karl Baden
50-51, 61: © John Drysdale
53, 64, 65: © Robin Schwartz
55: © Ned Rosen
57: © Johan Willner/Tiofoto
59, 62-63: © Ann Finnell
68, 69: Penguin/Corbis-Bettmann
77: © Marjorie Lundin/Tiofoto

Text: Jana Martin
Drawings: J.C. Suarès
Photo Research: Katrina Fried
Design: Tania Garcia